SOCCER CHAMPIONS

BY JIM WHITING

BAYERN MUNICH

Published by Creative Education
and Creative Paperbacks
P.O. Box 227, Mankato, Minnesota 56002
Creative Education and Creative Paperbacks
are imprints of The Creative Company
www.thecreativecompany.us

Design and production by The Design Lab
Art direction by Rita Marshall
Printed in Malaysia

Photographs by Corbis (YAHYA ARHAB/epa, Matthew
Ashton/AMA/Matthew Ashton/AMA/AMA, FABRIZIO
BENSCH/Reuters, Bettmann, Chris Brunskill, Corbis,
Cui Xinyu/Xinhua Press, dpa, Hulton-Deutsch Collection,
Frank Mächler/dpa, TOBY MELVILLE/Reuters, Sampics,
Universal/TempSport), Getty Images (Bongarts, Bob
Thomas), Logopedia (Unknown), photosinbox.com,
Shutterstock (gualtiero boffi, S.Borisov, Fingerhut, gary718,
Denis Kuvaev, mrHanson, Sean Pavone, Laszlo Szirtesi,
Yuri Turkov), Wikimedia Creative Commons (Unknown)

Library of Congress Cataloging-in-Publication Data
Whiting, Jim.
Bayern Munich / by Jim Whiting.
p. cm. — (Soccer champions)
Includes bibliographical references and index.
Summary: A chronicle of the people, matches,
and world events that shaped the European
men's German soccer team known as Bayern
Munich, from its founding in 1900 to today.
ISBN 978-1-60818-587-0 (hardcover)
ISBN 978-1-62832-192-0 (pbk)
1. FC Bayern (Soccer team)—History—
Juvenile literature. I. Title.

GV943.6.F36W45 2015
796.334'640943364—dc23   2014029642

CCSS: RI.5.1, 2, 3, 8; RH.6-8.4, 5, 7

First Edition HC 9 8 7 6 5 4 3 2 1
First Edition PBK 9 8 7 6 5 4 3 2 1

Cover and page 3: Winger Arjen Robben
Page 1: 2012 UEFA Champions League final

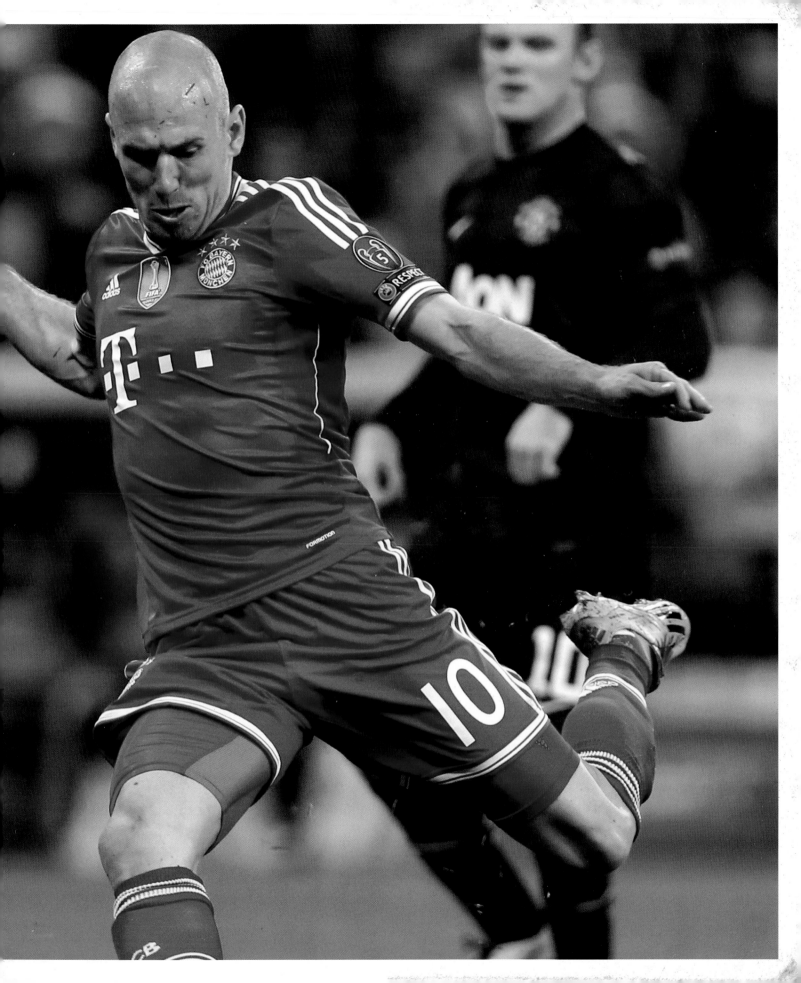

Goalkeeper Manuel Neuer

INTRODUCTION

Soccer (or football, as it is known almost everywhere else in the world) is truly a universal game. Nowhere is the play more competitive than in Europe. Almost every European country has its own league, and generally that league has several divisions. A typical season lasts eight or nine months, from late summer to mid-spring. Every team in each level plays all other teams in its level twice, once at home and once on the other team's pitch. At the end of the season, the bottommost teams in one division are relegated (moved down) to the next lower division, with the same number of topmost teams from that lower division promoted to replace them. Such a system ensures that a high level of competition is maintained and that late-season games between teams with losing records remain important as they seek to avoid relegation.

Individual countries also feature their own tournaments, such as England's FA Cup and Spain's Copa del Rey. In theory, these tournaments allow almost any team the opportunity to win the championship, but in reality the best clubs dominate the competition. An assortment of European-wide tournaments complement individual nations' league and cup play. The most prestigious is the Union of European Football Associations (UEFA) Champions League. Known as the European Cup until

Germany's Bayern Munich football club has proven itself on both the national and international stage.

1993, the Champions League is a tournament consisting of 32 teams drawn primarily from the highest finishers in the strongest national leagues. Other teams can play their way into the tournament in preliminary rounds. It originated in 1954, when the otherwise obscure Wolverhampton Wanderers of England defeated Honved, the top-rated Hungarian side, prompting Wanderers manager Stan Cullis to declare his team "Champions of the World." Noted French soccer journalist Gabriel Hanot disagreed and helped organize a continent-wide competition that began in 1956.

The Champions League starts with eight four-team pools, which play two games with one another. The top two teams from each pool begin a series of knockout rounds, also contested on a two-game basis. The last two teams play a single championship game at a neutral site. The tournament runs concurrently with league play, beginning in September and concluding in May. Teams that win their league, their national cup, and the Champions League during the same season are said to have won the Continental Treble—almost certainly the most difficult feat in all of professional sports. The winner of the Champions League is eligible for the FIFA Club World Cup, an annual seven-team tournament that originated in 2000. It also includes teams from the Americas and Caribbean, Africa, Asia, Oceania, and the host nation.

The other major European club championship is the UEFA Europa League, founded in 1971 and known as the UEFA Cup until the 2009–10 season. The winners of these two tournaments play for the UEFA Super Cup, usually held in August.

ALL-TIME CHAMPIONS LEAGUE RECORDS OF THE TOP 10 CLUBS (AS OF 2014):

	Winner	Runner-up
Real Madrid (Spain)	10	3
AC Milan (Italy)	7	4
Bayern Munich (Germany)	5	5
Liverpool (England)	5	2
Barcelona (Spain)	4	3
Ajax (Netherlands)	4	2
Manchester United (England)	3	2
Inter Milan (Italy)	3	2
Benfica (Portugal)	2	5
Juventus (Italy)	2	5

Allianz Arena

CONTINENTAL TREBLE WINNERS

Celtic (Scotland)	1966–67
Ajax (Netherlands)	1971–72
PSV (Netherlands)	1987–88
Manchester United (England)	1998–99
Barcelona (Spain)	2008–09
Inter Milan (Italy)	2009–10
Bayern Munich (Germany)	2012–13

TURNING AWAY FROM THE *TURNVEREIN*

Founded by Duke Henry the Lion in 1158, the city of Munich, Germany, grew rapidly. By 1506, it had become the capital of the southern German kingdom of Bavaria (also known as Bayern). Perhaps the most notable Bavarian ruler was "Mad King" Ludwig II, who took the throne in 1864 at the age of 18 and became renowned for such extravagant building projects as Neuschwanstein Castle. Bavaria joined the new German nation in 1871 and is today perhaps Germany's most prosperous region.

The fairy-tale-like Neuschwanstein Castle, located in the Bavarian Alps, welcomes 1.3 million tourists each year.

Famous Gothic structures in Munich's central square include the New Town Hall and Frauenkirche cathedral.

Munich shares in that prosperity and is especially noted for its culture. It boasts a number of world-famous cathedrals, civic structures, palaces, and art museums.

During the 19th century, Munich—like many German cities—established a *turnverein*, or gymnastics-oriented sports center. At a meeting in February 1900, the Munich turnverein's leaders refused to allow its soccer-playing members to join the newly formed Verband Sueddeutscher Fussball-Vereine (Association of South German Football Clubs, or SFV). In reference to its origins in England in the mid-1860s, many Germans dismissed the game as "the English disease." A prominent educator of the era named Otto Jaeger said, "We kick a vicious dog, and it is because this dog-kick plays such a huge role in football that I loathe the game, also because of the pitiful, crouching stance in which the players chase the ball."

Nevertheless, the game was catching on. About a dozen soccer enthusiasts led by Franz John left the turnverein and promptly formed their own club, which they named Bayern Munich. A few weeks later, the team won its first game, defeating another Munich club 5–2. That win set the tone for Bayern Munich's success for more than a decade. Playing in a variety of leagues, the team finished first or second every year.

The most notable player during the team's formative years was right-winger Max Gablonsky. Speedy enough to be named to the German 4x100 relay team in the 1912 Olympics, Gablonsky played three seasons for the German national team. He went on to play more than 500 games for Bayern before retiring in 1922.

When Germany entered World War I in 1914, soccer players were among those who volunteered or were forced to join the German Army. Even if they could scrape together a team, the few club soccer players who remained behind struggled to find places to play. Because a British naval blockade of Germany during the war prevented food and other supplies from entering the country, Kaiser Wilhelm II ordered that open spaces—including soccer fields—be plowed and used to grow potatoes.

Soon after the troops returned home in 1919, MTK, a Hungarian team, crushed Bayern 7–1. Kurt Landauer, Bayern's president, was so impressed with MTK that he not only tried to imitate their style of play—relying on creativity and quick passing—but also recruited some of their players and coaches. The newcomers helped Bayern make its mark. The team won numerous regional competitions and then took SFV titles in 1926 and 1928. A key contributor was defender Ludwig Goldbrunner, a Munich native who played his entire 18-year career in his hometown.

A star emerged in 1930 when 18-year-old striker Oskar Rohr joined the team. Rohr helped Bayern win the German championship in the 1931–32 season. But when the team became much less competitive the following year, Rohr decided to take his talents to another club.

During World War I, many German soldiers found themselves engaged in brutal trench warfare.

DESCENT INTO DARKNESS

One reason for the team's problems was Adolf Hitler's rise to national power at the head of the Nazi Party in 1933. Hitler was viciously anti-Semitic, which meant he was very prejudiced against Jews. Within a few months of his appointment as chancellor (leader of the German government), Jews were excluded from Germany's sports organizations as part of a policy known as *Gleichschaltung* (forcing into line). Hitler had spent much of his life in Munich. He especially disliked Bayern and dismissed it as the "Jewish Club." And indeed, two founders had been Jewish. So were Landauer and Richard Kohn, coach of the 1932 championship team.

At Hitler's orders, the Bayern team was relegated to a lower level of competition.

Unlike most German soccer teams that embraced Nazism, Bayern resisted and rebelled courageously against the racist and increasingly brutal policies of the Nazis. Once, team members fought a group of Hitler's thugs in a street brawl. The Nazis loved over-the-top pageantry, so fullback Sigmund Haringer was nearly thrown in prison for publicly sneering that a Nazi flag parade was "kids' theater." When African American sprinter Jesse Owens outraged Hitler by winning several gold medals in the 1936 Berlin Summer Olympics, Willy Simetsreiter—a

In the 1930s, all German citizens — even soccer players — were expected to hail Hitler (opposite) with the Nazi salute (above).

Bayern winger who was also a member of Germany's Olympic soccer team—posed for a picture with Owens. Three years later, as World War II began, Bayern captain Konrad Heidkamp buried the team's silverware and trophies on a farm when officials called for all precious metals to be donated to the German war effort. And when Bayern played a game in neutral Switzerland in 1943, the team lined up and waved to club president Landauer, who had lived in exile there for several years. This small act of defiance occurred in front of members of the Gestapo, the German secret police, who accompanied the team.

In retaliation for their resistance, several Bayern members were conscripted into the army and sent to the Eastern Front to fight against the Soviet Union. Teams more receptive to Nazi control, such as TSV 1860 Munich, received favorable treatment. Winger Franz Krumm, who scored a goal in the 1932 championship game, was among the casualties on the Eastern Front. He was killed in action in 1943. Still, Bayern continued to play, and on April 23, 1945—the final recorded soccer game in Germany before Hitler committed suicide and the war in Europe came to a close—they defeated 1860 Munich.

The immediate aftermath of the war was difficult for German soccer. Many pitches had been cratered by falling bombs. Even finding a ball was sometimes

Heavy Allied bombing throughout World War II left Cologne and other major German cities in ruins.

problematic. This situation was part of a much larger picture of desolation in Germany. Most cities were heavily damaged, and food was scarce. In one notable example of postwar survival, powerful FC Nürnberg traveled to the tiny town of Altötting to play the local team in exchange for a butchered pig. Clothing was also hard to come by. Some teams even used Nazi flags—with the swastika symbol removed—as material for their uniforms.

Another hindrance was that the victorious Allied powers—the Soviet Union, United States, Great Britain, and France—had divided Germany among themselves. They were reluctant to allow large public gatherings. Nevertheless, the Oberliga Süd was founded in 1945 as a league for clubs—such as Bayern—within U.S.-occupied southern Germany. During its 18 years in the league, Bayern's best finish was third, a mark achieved 4 times. The team came

in last in 1954–55 and was relegated. Forward Peter Velhorn's 19 goals the following season helped Bayern to a second-place finish in its division and promotion back to the league's top level. Bayern won the DFB-Pokal—the German Cup—in 1957, its first championship in 25 years. Forward Rudi Jobst scored the game's only goal in the final against Fortuna Düsseldorf of western Germany.

The watershed moment in German soccer came in 1963 with the establishment of a national league called the Bundesliga. However, Bayern wasn't included among the 16 original teams. The new organization didn't want two teams from the same city. Since 1860 Munich had won the Oberliga Süd in 1962–63, they became the city's representative in the Bundesliga. Bayern joined the Regionalliga Süd, Germany's second-highest level of play.

BAYERN BECOMES A FORCE

When the league expanded to 18 teams 2 seasons later, Bayern was admitted. By then they had amassed a formidable nucleus: striker Gerd Müller, sweeper Franz Beckenbauer, and keeper Sepp Maier—a free spirit who once spent several minutes during a game chasing a duck that wandered onto the pitch. The team was in title contention for the entire 1965–66 season, finishing just three points behind 1860 Munich, then capturing the DFB-Pokal. That win qualified Bayern for the European Cup Winners' Cup, in which the club defeated the Glasgow Rangers in the final for the first of many international trophies.

A talented roster helped Bayern overcome a scoreless regulation and capture the 1967 European Cup Winners' Cup final.

The 1972 Summer Olympics at Munich's Olympiastadion were blighted by the terrorist killings of Israeli athletes.

With its core players benefiting from several years' worth of experience, Bayern burst out of the gate to start the 1968–69 Bundesliga season and never looked back. The eight-point margin it held over runner-up Alemannia Aachen in the final standings was the league's largest to that point. For good measure, Bayern added the DFB-Pokal with a 2–1 triumph over FC Schalke 04. The team hit its stride in the early 1970s, winning three Bundesliga titles in a row and adding another DFB-Pokal.

In 1972, the team moved to the state-of-the-art Olympiastadion, built for the ill-fated Munich Olympics that year. Its 77,000-seat capacity almost doubled that of Grünwalder Stadion, the previous pitch, and was instrumental in helping Bayern become Germany's wealthiest club.

By that time, it had also become the nation's most hated club. While the reasons aren't entirely clear for the intense feelings of dislike Bayern players experienced, soccer historian Uli Hesse observes that, "Only Bayern could cross the country and still find themselves physically attacked." For instance, on the last day of the 1970–71 season, the club traveled to Duisburg, needing a win to secure the Bundesliga title.

Spurred on by their fans, the Duisburg side played with an intensity that suggested they were the ones with something to gain and emerged with a 2–0 triumph. As the Bayern players jogged off the field, they were roundly jeered by the spectators, even though Beckenbauer and Maier had been heroes during the previous year as West Germany took third in the World Cup.

On another occasion, a mob in Oberhausen surrounded team members as they headed for their bus after a game and threw trash at them. "It was an eerie feeling," Maier said. "Like lynch justice in the Wild West." Hard-nosed defender Franz "The Bull" Roth lived up to his name, throwing a few punches at the team's tormentors.

In 1974, Bayern made its first appearance in the finals of the European Cup (the earlier form of the Champions League). In a nail-biting finish, the team defeated Atlético de Madrid. Bayern's good fortune in the Cup finals continued in the two

Despite its critics, Bayern won the European Cup trophy in 1974 (opposite) and 1975 (above).

following years. Playing against Leeds in 1975, Bayern benefited when what seemed an obvious foul in the penalty zone wasn't called. Then an apparent Leeds goal was disallowed. "We had a bit of luck when the referee disallowed an English goal," Beckenbauer said later. "Had the English team gone ahead and taken a 1–0 lead, I don't think we would have been able to turn the game around." Instead, Roth and Müller both tallied goals in the final 20 minutes for a 2–0 win.

With seemingly all of France looking on in 1976—St. Etienne was only the second French team to appear in the final in more than 20 years—Bayern maintained its good fortune as 2 St. Etienne shots hit the crossbar. Roth's 25-yard goal was the only score.

ONE ERA ENDS, ANOTHER BEGINS

But the heart of the team was aging, and by the end of the 1970s, Beckenbauer, Maier, and Müller had all departed. So had defender/midfielder Jupp Kapellmann and forward Uli Hoeness, who had been ideal complements to the team's superstars. Bayern tumbled off its perch at the top of the Bundesliga for several years. The run

Paul Breitner attracted nearly as much attention for his controversial beliefs as for his playing.

of success resumed in 1980, as Bayern won the Bundesliga seven times during the ensuing decade. One of the most recognizable stars of this era was midfielder/defender Paul Breitner, who sported an Afro, publicly stated his agreement with the political philosophy of Chinese communist leader Mao Zedong, and refused to sing the German national anthem before games. On the pitch, however, Breitner became one of the highest-scoring defenders in Bayern history, with more than 100 career goals.

For several years, the team was often referred to by its nickname of "FC Breitnigge," combining the names of Breitner and striker Karl-Heinz Rummenigge. Another key contributor during the 1980s era of success was hard-nosed sweeper/defender Klaus Augenthaler.

In 1981, Breitner was Germany's player of the year, while Rummenigge was the Bundesliga's top scorer.

Striker Dieter Hoeness (left) helped Bayern take on Porto in the 1987 European Cup final before retiring.

Bayern returned to the European Cup final in 1987, heavily favored to win against Porto of Portugal. Midfielder Ludwig Kögl put Bayern ahead 25 minutes into the game, and through much of the second half, it appeared as though the score would stand. But Porto striker Rabah Madjer backfooted the ball into the goal to tie the game, and moments later, Brazilian-born forward Juary volleyed home the winning shot for Porto. Soccer fans throughout the world had little sympathy for Bayern's crushing loss. As Hesse explains, "By this time, just about everybody had become sick to the core of Bayern Munich, the football club that always won. Or almost always." Bayern's success was due, in part, to its habit of using its considerable wealth to buy promising young talent from other Bundesliga teams.

Despite the stacked roster and a runner-up finish in the 1990–91 Bundesliga, the wheels came off in 1991–92. The team finished 10th in the Bundesliga and was 5 points from being relegated—something seemingly impossible for a club with Bayern's pedigree and prestige. Two coaches were fired. As Hesse notes, "It was the first year the club really started becoming 'FC Hollywood'—a headline-generating machine that was a dream come true for the tabloid press." One player borrowed a teammate's car without permission and wrecked it. Another seemed to spend more time on the golf course than in training. A third was suspended after a restaurant brawl. A fourth dragged his relationship with his beauty-queen girlfriend through the media. It also didn't help that three Bayern members of the 1990 German World Cup-winning team—Augenthaler, Jurgen Kohler, and Stefan Reuter—left before the season began. Almost unbelievably, Bayern lost 6 of its first 14 games in 1991–92, quickly exited DFB-Pokal play with a home loss to second-division FC Homburg 4-2, and then suffered a 6–2 rout by Copenhagen in the UEFA Cup. Some people believed that Bayern's dominance had finally come to an end.

The club rebounded the following season to finish second, a point behind league titlist Werder Bremen, and took the top spot in 1993–94. A notable addition came in 1995 when forward Jürgen Klinsmann joined the team. Bayern won the 1996–97 Bundesliga and remained in the league's upper reaches from then on.

In 1999, Bayern faced England's Manchester United in its first appearance in the finals of what was now known as the Champions League since its loss to Porto 12 years earlier. Bayern winger Mario Basler slammed home a curving penalty kick just six minutes into the match. The Germans continued to control the field, and only two shots that hit the goalposts kept them from putting the game away. But then, in an echo of the 1987 European Cup loss, Manchester scored twice in the final moments of second-half stoppage time, leaving the Germans stunned. "It was a very bitter moment," said Bayern coach Ottmar Hitzfeld, "but you have to realize that in sport anything is possible and the opponents that day had more luck and we made mistakes, and when you do that, you get punished."

Two years later, it was Bayern's turn to do the punishing. After eliminating Manchester United in the quarterfinals and defending champion Real Madrid in the semis, Bayern defeated Valencia CF of Spain through sudden-death penalty kicks to secure its fourth Champions League title.

After a disappointing record in Champions League finals, Bayern finally redeemed itself in 2001.

BAYERN DOMINATES THE BUNDESLIGA

Allianz Arena is home to Munich's rival clubs but is lit in blue for 1860 Munich games.

The club moved into its new home, Allianz Arena, in 2005. Regarded as the most modern soccer stadium in Europe, Allianz is especially distinctive for its façade of 2,760 diamond-shaped panels that glow red in the evening. Bayern's proven record of success helped draw spectators to Allianz, and the nearly 70,000 seats were almost always filled.

By now it was clear that Bayern—not considered good enough to join the Bundesliga at its formation—was the league's dominant team, often winning the championship or being runner-up. The situation was the same in the DFB-Pokal. Bayern took both titles six times between 2000 and 2010.

Bayern's team effort couldn't overcome Inter's quick-counterattack strategy in the 2010 Champions League final.

When Bayern and Italy's Inter Milan met in the 2010 Champions League final, the winner would become the first team from its country to win the Continental Treble—the league, national cup, and Champions League titles. Though Bayern had more than a two-to-one edge in time of possession, Inter scored a 2–0 win. More Champions League heartbreak was in store for 2012. Playing against England's Chelsea in Allianz Arena—which had long been designated as host—Bayern finally broke through in the 83rd minute on an unusual goal. Thomas Müller—a versatile player capable of attacking as a winger, midfielder, and second striker—headed a crossing pass into the ground in front of the goal. It bounced over the keeper's head and caromed off the crossbar into the net. But in another grim repeat of 1987's and 1999's outcome, Chelsea retaliated in the 88th minute to knot the score. When Bayern winger Arjen Robben missed a penalty kick in extra time, the game came down to

a shootout. Chelsea converted 4 tries to Bayern's 3. "After the [Champions League] final in 2012, we had two options: the team could either break apart or grow closer together," team captain Philipp Lahm explained.

It didn't take long to see which option the team had chosen. The year 2013 was the greatest in club history, perhaps the greatest year for any club team. Bayern clinched the 2012–13 Bundesliga title on April 6—by far the earliest in league history. The team scored 98 goals in 34 games while allowing just 18, a league-record 80-goal differential. After destroying powerful FC Barcelona 4–0 and 3–0 in a widely anticipated Champions League semifinal, Bayern took on FC Dortmund in the first-ever all-German final. With Dortmund dominating play for much of the first half, Bayern keeper Manuel Neuer made five key saves to preserve a scoreless

An evenly fought battle on the pitch for the 2013 UEFA Super Cup title came down to penalty kicks.

tie. Bayern striker Mario Mandžukić broke the deadlock in the 60th minute, though Dortmund tied the score 8 minutes later. This time it was Bayern that scored in the final moments. Robben poked a back-heeled pass from winger Franck Ribéry into the net for a 2–1 victory. A week later, the team knocked off VfB Stuttgart 3–2 to take the DFB-Pokal and become the first German team (and only the seventh overall) to win the coveted Continental Treble.

There was more to come. In August, Bayern gained revenge against Chelsea in UEFA's Super Cup final in a match eerily reminiscent of the Champions League final the previous year—only with the result reversed. After a 1–1 tie in regular time, Chelsea took the lead in extra time, but Javi Martínez's equalizing goal in the waning moments forced a shootout, which Bayern won 5–4.

Franck Ribéry's (right) performance earned him Player of the Tournament honors at the 2013 FIFA Club World Cup.

To cap the year, Bayern defeated Raja Casablanca 2–0 on December 21 to capture the FIFA Club World Cup—its fifth major trophy. The nimble center defender known simply as Dante scored just 7 minutes into the contest, and central midfielder Thiago Alcântara netted the second goal 15 minutes later. "It was easy to summon up the energy needed to compete there, and it made for the perfect end to an unbelievable year," Lahm said.

Bayern stretched its Bundesliga unbeaten streak to 53, finally losing to Augsburg on April 5, 2014. With the title in hand, though, several young players got the chance to start as Bayern finished out the season. Many observers felt that the team would win its second straight Continental Treble. However, a shocking 4–0 home loss to Real Madrid in the Champions League semifinals kept that from happening. Bayern rebounded to defeat Borussia Dortmund 2–0 to capture the DFB-Pokal. This marked the team's 10th German Double (winning the Bundesliga and DFB-Pokal in the same season) ever.

Bayern's place as one of the brightest stars in all the European soccer firmament seemed cemented. As of 2015, it had 23 Bundesliga titles (as compared with 5 for the next closest team) and 17 DFB-Pokals (versus 6 for the runner-up). Bayern also maintained a massive fan base—and at least an equal number of detractors who continued the decades-long tradition of hoping the Bavarian giant fell hard. "We cultivate this polarization," said Karl-Heinz Rummenigge, Bayern's CEO since 2002. "Partly because it means that we have constant media exposure."

Continued winning is another key element in maintaining a high level of media exposure. To achieve this goal, the team constantly develops young talent such as defender David Alaba. At the age of 17, Alaba became the youngest-ever member of Austria's national team. Thomas Müller, who joined Bayern's youth program when he was 10, captured the spotlight when he won the Golden Boot award at the 2010 World Cup. In 2014, Bayern added Dortmund striker Robert Lewandowski. "Lewandowski is a super player," said Robben, who, as the 2010 European Footballer of the Year, knew quite a bit about talent. "He is really good. He's one of the world's best strikers. Our squad will be even better."

And that has to be bad news for every other German team—to say nothing of the rest of Europe. Bayern Munich has endured several potholes on its road to becoming one of the world's elite club teams. Now it purrs along like a high-performance German car on a smooth highway with no end in sight.

In addition to his offensive runs, David Alaba (right) proved capable of aggressive defense and well-timed tackles.

MEMORABLE MATCHES

1900

Team was founded.

1932

Bayern Munich v. Eintracht Frankfurt

German Championships, June 12, 1932, Nuremberg, Germany

After finishing as the Southern German runner-up, Bayern Munich qualified for the German championships for the first time. The team defeated Minerva 93 Berlin 4–2 in the opening round of the tournament, Polizei SV Chemnitz 3–2 in the quarterfinals, and FC Nürnberg 2–0 in the semis. The title game was a repeat of the Southern German championship six weeks earlier, which Eintracht Frankfurt had won 2–0. Bayern's Oskar Rohr opened the scoring soon after the 30-minute mark with a short free kick. "Shortly before hitting the ball, Rohr's foot touched the ground … causing the kick to be placed above the Eintracht keeper in the back of the net," recounts soccer blogger Niklas Wildhagen. "It is still believed that Rohr's kick would have hit [Eintracht keeper] Schmitt straight in his stomach instead of going over him had Rohr's foot not slithered across grass." Winger Franz Krumm sealed the win with a goal at 75 minutes. The 2–0 triumph would remain the high point for Bayern Munich for the next 25 years.

1967

Bayern Munich v. Glasgow Rangers

European Cup Winners' Cup, May 31, 1967, Nuremberg, Germany

Winning the 1966 DFB-Pokal qualified Bayern for the 1967 European Cup Winners' Cup, the team's first international competition. The four preliminary rounds featured two games apiece, with Bayern winning the first three by a single goal on aggregate (the goals scored in the two games). The semis were easier, as Bayern defeated Standard Liège of Belgium 5–1. In the final, the team faced the Rangers. The Rangers' archrival Celtic (another Glasgow team) had won the European Cup (an earlier name for the Champions League) the previous week, so Scottish fans hoped for a double (winning two major titles). The game was held in the Bavarian city of Nuremberg, with nearly all the 70,000 fans pulling for Bayern. In a tight defensive struggle, the Scots dominated the first half—punching in a disallowed goal—while Bayern controlled the second half. Neither team could score, so the game went into extra time. In the 109th minute, Bayern midfielder Franz Roth, nicknamed "the Bull" for his physical style of play, looped the game-winner over Rangers keeper Norrie Martin. Eleven days later, Bayern shut out Hamburger SV 4–0 to win the DFB-Pokal again.

1974

Bayern Munich v. Atlético de Madrid

European Cup Final, May 15, 1974, Brussels, Belgium

In its first appearance in a European Cup final, Bayern kept pace with opponent Atlético de Madrid throughout regulation time. In extra time, a free kick put Atlético ahead with six minutes remaining. With less than 30 seconds left, Gerd Müller—the tournament's leading scorer—found himself momentarily in the clear. He waved frantically to defender Hans-Georg Schwarzenbeck to pass him the ball. Though he was nearly 30 yards from the goal, Schwarzenbeck launched the soccer equivalent of an American football "Hail Mary" through a swarm of players. Somehow the ball eluded Atlético keeper Miguel Reina. According to legend, Reina had been distracted by a photographer behind the goal who had asked for his jersey. Under the rules in place at that time, the 1–1 tie forced a replay of the entire game two days later. Bayern then buried the Spaniards 4–0, beginning its three-year domination of the Cup. According to soccer writer Raphael Honigstein, Schwarzenbeck scored "the most important goal in the history of the club, perhaps of any club." Scoring was a rarity for Schwarzenbeck, who tallied only 29 other goals in his 14-year Bayern career.

1982

Bayern Munich v. Aston Villa

European Cup Final, May 26, 1982, Rotterdam, Netherlands

Boasting a seasoned core of players, Bayern was heavily favored to win its fourth European Cup against an Aston Villa side that had finished 11th in its league. Things seemed even worse for the English when their keeper had to leave the game less than 10 minutes after it started. His replacement, Nigel Spink, had played in only one First Division game—a loss three years earlier. Aston Villa played solid defense to give Spink enough time to settle in before Bayern began peppering him. He made two acrobatic saves, but Bayern maintained the pressure. In the 67th minute, 2 Bayern defenders converged on winger Tony Morley running down the left side, leaving forward Peter Withe unmarked in front of the goal. Morley's pass found Withe, who tapped it past keeper Manfred Müller. Though the Germans rallied to score in the 88th minute, they looked on in horror as the referee raised his hand to indicate offside. Aston's 1–0 victory is one of the greatest-ever upsets in Champions League history.

2001

Bayern Munich v. Valencia CF
Champions League Final, May 23, 2001, Milan, Italy

Fresh with bitter memories of last-minute defeats in its 2 most recent appearances in the finals, Bayern was still favored to win its fourth Champions League title in 2001 after a 25-year drought. However, a Valencia free kick just two minutes into the game gave considerable momentum to the Spaniards. Their confidence increased when Valencia keeper Santiago Cañizares blocked midfielder Mehmet Scholl's penalty kick five minutes later. In the 50th minute, Bayern midfielder Stefan Effenberg supplied the equalizer on yet another penalty kick. Though Bayern dominated the remainder of the match, it had to settle for a 1–1 tie at the end of regulation and extra time. The shootout that followed left the teams tied 3–3 after the first round. Thomas Linke scored for Bayern to open the second sudden-death round. Bayern keeper Oliver Kahn—already with two saves—faced Valencia's Mauricio Pellegrino. Sepp Maier, Bayern's keeper coach and a mainstay of the superb teams of the mid-1970s, said, "[Kahn] has shown over the last few years that he is a world-class goalkeeper." Kahn lived up to Maier's praise, diving to his right and swatting the ball away to give Bayern the 5–4 win.

2013

Bayern Munich v. FC Augsburg
Bundesliga, November 9, 2013, Munich, Germany

When Bayern notched a win on November 2, 2013, it marked the team's 36th consecutive Bundesliga game without a loss. That streak equaled a 30-year-old standard set by Hamburger SV in 1983. Bayern hadn't lost since October 2012, its only defeat in the 2012–13 season en route to winning the Bundesliga by a whopping 25 points. Playing before a lively home crowd, Bayern seemed motivated to extend the streak and establish a new record. Left unmarked near the goal, Bayern defender Jérôme Boateng powered a kick into the top of the net four minutes into the game. Augsburg narrowly escaped further damage when defender David Alaba's free kick sailed just over the bar. Then Augsburg keeper Marwin Hitz smothered a hard shot by defender Dante. But left-winger Franck Ribéry's direct free kick shortly before halftime gave Bayern a 2–0 edge and all but sealed the victory. In the final minute of the second half, Thomas Müller added icing to the record-setting cake by converting a free kick. Bayern stretched its unbeaten streak to 53 games before finally losing (1–0) to none other than Augsburg on April 5, 2014.

FAMOUS FOOTBALLERS

OSKAR ROHR

(1912–88)
Striker, 1930–33

Rohr joined Bayern Munich in 1930 when he was just 18. A gifted and quick striker, "Ossi" played a key role in Bayern's 1932 German championship. He also scored five goals in four games with the German national team. In Rohr's day, German soccer players couldn't make a living in their sport. So Rohr left Munich after the 1932–33 season and signed a pro contract with the Swiss team Grasshopper Zurich. Although he helped his new team win the Swiss Cup that year, the German press treated him with contempt. When Rohr moved to FC Strasbourg in 1934, the magazine *Kicker* said, "A huge talent as a player—but, his character? There are no good things to be said about somebody who betrayed his Vaterland [fatherland]." A star with Strasbourg, Rohr lived very well until the German Army occupied France in 1940. Enraged by his "betrayal," German officials with long memories sent him to a concentration camp. Then he was forced to join the German Army. He managed to survive and played four years after the war for several German teams.

KURT LANDAUER

(1884–1961)
Player, 1901–02 (?)
President, 1913–14, 1919–33, 1947–51

As a young man, Kurt Landauer played for Bayern until he moved to Switzerland to enter the banking profession. He returned to Munich in 1905, continued playing, then assumed the club presidency in 1913. When World War I began the following year, he joined the German Army. After the war, Landauer resumed his post with Bayern, bringing energy and financial success to the team. His knowledge of business made the team increasingly successful. He was especially noted for opposing many members who wanted to build a stadium. Instead, Landauer invested in the club's youth program. His tenure reached its highest point in 1932 when Bayern won its first German championship. He had to resign the following year because of accusations that Bayern was a "Jewish club." Landauer was arrested in 1939 and sent to the Dachau concentration camp near Munich. His service in World War I resulted in his release a month later, and he fled to Switzerland for his safety. He returned to Munich in 1947 to serve a final four-year term as club president. In 2013, he was named an honorary club president in recognition of his legacy. "His efforts were pioneering during an extremely difficult time for FC Bayern," said Bayern CEO Karl-Heinz Rummenigge.

GERD MÜLLER

(1945–)
Striker, 1964–79

Even though he was called "kleines dickes Müller" ("short fat Müller") by his first Bayern coach (who also asked, "What am I supposed to do with a weightlifter?"), Gerd Müller's much more fitting nickname was "Bomber der Nation" ("the Nation's Bomber"). As author David Winner notes, "Müller was short, squat, awkward-looking, and not notably fast; he never fit the conventional idea of a great footballer, but he had lethal acceleration over short distances, a remarkable aerial game, and uncanny goal-scoring instincts. His short legs gave him a strangely low center of gravity, so he could turn quickly." Müller used those features to his advantage, scoring 398 goals in 453 appearances during his 15-season Bayern career. He led the Bundesliga in scoring 7 times, and his 40 goals in 1971–72 remain the league's single-season record. With the West German national team, he was even more deadly, racking up 68 goals in 62 games. His 1972 record of 85 goals scored during a calendar year wasn't broken until 2012. Müller remains highly regarded today, with the Adidas athletic company featuring soccer shoes bearing his name and a line of "Der Bomber" apparel.

FRANZ BECKENBAUER

(1945–)
Sweeper, 1964–77

Generally regarded as Germany's best player ever, Franz Beckenbauer showed signs of greatness in 1958 as a 13-year-old. Because TSV 1860 Munich was the city's most popular club at the time, it

seemed likely that Beckenbauer would join them. But playing in a youth game against 1860, Beckenbauer was decked by an opposing player. The furious teenager signed with Bayern instead and joined the parent club for the 1964–65 season. As a center-back, he experimented with mounting attacks from his position and in essence created the modern role of sweeper. According to the International Football Hall of Fame (IFHOF), "Those powerful long runs out of central defense had never been seen before. Up to then, no one had thought that a sweeper had any job being in his opponents' half of the field, let alone scoring…. It became his trademark." Beckenbauer remained with the team in several roles after his retirement in 1984, becoming honorary president in 2009. "There was an arrogance in his play that suggested he was always in command," the IFHOF remarked. "'Emperor Franz' and 'The Kaiser' they called him."

JÜRGEN KLINSMANN

(1964–)
Striker, 1995–97

Jürgen Klinsmann came to Bayern with a reputation as one of Germany's most prolific scorers. When he was 9, he scored 102 goals in his youth team's season, with 16 in a single game. By the time he played with West Germany's 1990 World Cup–winning team, his three goals made him even more famous. When he added five in 1994 and three in 1998, Klinsmann became the first player to score at least three times in three successive World Cups. Unsurprisingly, then, he led Bayern in scoring during his two-year tenure with the club. In his first season, the team won the UEFA Cup for the first time. Klinsmann scored 15 goals in the tournament's 12 games, a record that stood for 15 years. The following season, he helped Bayern win the Bundesliga. After his playing career, Klinsmann coached the German national team to third place in the 2006 World Cup, and then became the U.S. men's national team coach in 2011. The following year, the team had its best-ever winning percentage, including the first American victory over Italy since 1934. Klinsmann guided the team to the 2014 World Cup, in which the U.S. lost in the round of 16.

FRANCK RIBÉRY

(1983–)
Winger, 2007–present

From the moment Franck Ribéry joined Bayern, the French left wing dazzled fans with his energy and pinpoint passing. He began his pro career at the age of 13 with LOSC Lille and made his senior debut with Boulogne 3 years later. After helping Marseille to the finals of the Coupe de France in 2005–06 and 2006–07, Ribéry joined Bayern for the following season for a

then-club record 25 million-Euro transfer fee. His stellar play seemed to justify the expense. He has played in two World Cups and many additional games for the French national team. His career has attracted numerous accolades. In 2008, he became the first player to be named both French and German Football Player of the Year. Zinedine Zidane, who at one time was regarded as the top French player, called him "the jewel of French football." And a huge outdoor billboard in Munich pays homage to the city's royal past and sporting present. It depicts a crowned Ribéry in a flowing 19th-century ermine-tipped blue robe worn by King Ludwig II beside the phrase "Bavaria has a king again."

BAYERN MUNICH TITLES
THROUGH 2014

**EUROPEAN CUP/
CHAMPIONS
LEAGUE**

Winner
1974
1975
1976
2001
2013
Total: 5

Runner-up
1982
1987
1999
2010
2012
Total: 5

BUNDESLIGA

1968–69
1971–72
1972–73
1973–74
1979–80
1980–81
1984–85
1985–86
1986–87
1988–89
1989–90
1993–94
1996–97
1998–99
1999–2000
2000–01
2002–03
2004–05
2005–06
2007–08
2009–10
2012–13
2013–14
Total: 23

DFB-POKAL

1957
1966
1967
1969
1971
1982
1984
1986
1998
2000
2003
2005
2006
2008
2010
2013
2014
Total: 17

SELECTED BIBLIOGRAPHY

Goldblatt, David, and Johnny Acton. *The Soccer Book: The Sport, the Teams, the Tactics, the Cups.* New York: DK, 2010.

Hesse, Uli. *Tor! The Story of German Football.* London: WSC Books, 2011.

Radnedge, Keir. *The Ultimate Encyclopedia of European Soccer.* London: Carlton Books, 2002.

UEFA. *Champions of Europe, 1955–2005: 50 Years of the World's Greatest Club Football; The Best Goals from All 50 Finals.* DVD. Pleasanton, Calif.: Soccer Learning Systems, 2005.

WEBSITES

THE BUNDESLIGA
http://www.bundesliga.com/en/
The Bundesliga's official website covers information on all the league's
teams, from results and standings to news, video, and more.

FC BAYERN MUNICH
https://www.fcbayern.de/en/
Bayern Munich's official website, with news, features, photos, results, videos, and more.

Note: Every effort has been made to ensure that the websites listed above are suitable
for children, that they have educational value, and that they contain no inappropriate
material. However, because of the nature of the Internet, it is impossible to guarantee that
these sites will remain active indefinitely or that their contents will not be altered.

INDEX

DATE DUE
